For the greater glory of God

"If today you hear His voice harden
not your hearts"
Psalm 95:7-8

COME

FOLLOW

RELAX

Ginny Kearney Allen

Introduction

If prayer is the lifting up of our minds and hearts to God, and if it is a covenant relationship between God and man in Christ, then I would expect that, when I am willing to listen, God will answer or speak to me. Because of this belief I often take pen in hand, come to the Lord in quiet, and expect that He might answer me.

The following example may explain this more fully.

You need none of your senses to experience Me. Since you are open to Me, I come to you in a supernatural way. In this way we converse in the silence of your heart. Away from all distractions, in the midst of pain or heartache, in whatever place you find yourself ~ in a crowd or all alone - we have the opportunity to dialogue...

Hear Me when I call. Hear Me within your heart and your soul…Be alert. Your natural hearing is only one small way to be in touch….Listen and hear Me when I call. I call often.

8/28/98

I am a 73 year old female extrovert on natural and spiritual steroids, and am generally found talking. Recently I spent five days on a silent directed retreat in my old home town, Milton, Massachusetts. The silence was work and the time since returning has been even more work.

What follows is the result of the meditations that I was assigned. God does speak to us when we are silent and willing to listen. He has spoken to me often in the past. This time I felt I was to publish. At the top of each page will be a reference to a particular Bible verse. Use whatever Bible you prefer. Following this Bible reference are the words I believe God spoke to my heart in contemplation.

The correct term for this is Lectio Divina. Read a portion of scripture and move towards a conversation with God from your heart. Move into His wounds where He can transform you while you spend silent time with Jesus Christ and where you can be wide open and trust Him to heal and convert you.

Thank you for spending your time in reading this one page at a time. I would appreciate any comments when you have finished. I may be reached at:

Ginny K. Allen
255 Sea Road
Kennebunk, Maine 04043
Ginny-K-Allen@hotmail.com

Acknowledgements

Father Joseph H. Casey S.J.

Father Peter Gojuk OMV

Father Aurelijus Gricius OFM

Steve Gannaway

Bernadette Cyr

Annemariea Schmidt

~Barbara~Dot~Ethel~Heide~Jennie
~Kathy~Michelle~

All those who prayed and continue to
pray for me.

Dedication

Justin Mennis Laurence Kearney
"Chuck"
8/21/09-8/3/61

My every loving Daddy, who, in persona Christi for me, chipped away at my faults in a way that was painful and gentle and sculpted me into who I have become today

"For I believe, Ginny, that you are one of the finest persons I have ever known, with an integrity and strength of character and personality that is very rare, and for which I thank God every day of my life. My pride in you and my love for you go beyond any words I could ever find for expressing them.

My problem is that I seek perfection in one I love so very deeply and of whom I am so proud. I am like a sculptor who tries to improve on a

masterpiece by chipping, chipping
away at small imperfections,
neglecting the beauty of the whole.
Thus I keep carping on your small
faults and forget to mention all your
wonderful virtues.
So, please, Ginny, forgive your loving
father for all his faults, for all the
times he has hurt you, and try to
remember only his deep love for you
and his unbounded pride in his
wonderful daughter." July 20, 1960

Listen
I will speak deep in your heart
I will help you plumb the depths
Hold on tightly
The going may be slippery
Be not afraid

Feel My Presence
Keep this with you
I will never leave you
You can count on Me
I am always with you
Let go of the tensions
Let go of trying to play Me
I am God
There is no other
Bring them to Me in prayer
If I need more from you
I will let you know
Be still and know that I Am God
Relax-enjoy yourself
I am in charge and in control

~Genesis Chapter 1~

I said increase and multiply
You obeyed
I created all
I created you
I sustain you
I love you
Do My will
Listen more carefully
Think before speaking
Pause and reflect before responding
Allow Me to show you who you really
are
Allow Me to grow you
I have asked you to stop squirming
Obey Me
You understand obedience
Don't question Me
Just do what I ask of you

~Psalm 104~

I alone am God
I Am Three in One
I always was and always will be
I care for all
I care for you
Do not worry
Relax-rest-and allow Me to love you

~Psalm 139~

Don't worry about Me
I don't need protection
You do
I protect you
I hem you in
I care for you
No evil can touch Me
I protect you from evil
See My protection
Feel My protection
Allow Me to enfold and envelop you
I caress you like a hug
I keep you warm like a coat
I keep you from harm like a fierce dog
You are Mine
I want you with Me in eternity
Allow Me to show you My way.

~Psalm 43:1-7~

Trust in Me
Allow Me to lead
Hold tightly to My hand
This way you cannot stray
Remember your Daddy
He never caused you harm
You trusted him
He was in persona Christi for you
Remember his words to and about you
He loved you
I love you even more
I am your Jesus mercy
Let it coat you
Let it envelope you
Let it fill you
Come away with Me
Come into My silence
Learn from Me, I will set you free
You need to be freed from yourself
Let it all go
Fall into My arms and rest in Me

Isaiah 49:14-16, 46:3ff~

Your Mother's pain was deep
She did the best she could
She loved Me
She asked Me to care for you
I did
You are special
You are loved
I have showered you with gifts
You have not always recognized them
Never have you been unprotected
Never have you been left alone
I was present before your birth
I was there during the trauma
You were bathed in prayer
You have always been Mine
Stop struggling
There is no war to fight
There is no need for flight
Relax and enjoy the world around
you
Open your eyes and ears to life
Let it all in

I will not allow you to be
overwhelmed
I will not desert or abandon you
Stop setting yourself up to be
abandoned
Be discreet-discern-be polite
People will come to you
Stop looking for them
I will send them
Now is the time to be free
Rejoice-relax-recreate

~Isaiah 55~

All is not lost
Everything can be recovered
Come to Me
Ask of Me
All is yours for the asking
I refresh you
I console you during your trials
I give you rest in Me
I will never leave you nor forsake you
All roads are not barren
All are not dead ends
Return now to the highway   to heaven
Stop going across the road
Remain with Me
I am heading in the right direction
I Am The Way

~Exodus 3:1-6~

I came to Moses while he was minding
his own business
I showed Myself to him
He was not expecting Me
I surprised him
Be open to surprises

~Psalm 103~

I bless those who obey Me
I show them My way
I travel with them
I hold them
I may carry them
I offer them fulfillment
I offer them joy and peace
I allow them pain and sorrow
I share Myself with them

~Psalm 63~

Long for Me
I wait for you
Trust in Me
I give you My love
Linger with Me and love Me

~Luke 11:1-13~

I give when you ask
Ask in My will
Learn to discern My will
I do not give what would harm you
I give only the best
Often you may need to wait
Patience is a virtue
You will receive whatever you need

~Luke 15:11-32~

My Mercy is yours
You have always been blessed by it
You didn't understand it
I showered it on you
This is the gist of your Daddy's
prayer
It was and is his legacy to you
Because you have mercy; you are
willing and able to extend it
Recognize that the more I shower on
you
The more you are called to distribute it

~ Luke 10:29-37 ~

Who was the man on the side of the
road?
Was he rich or poor?
Was he short or tall?
Was he laborer or servant?
I didn't and don't tell you
He was stripped naked
He was penniless
He was every man and no man
He was precious in My sight
He was one of my children
He did not deserve to be shamed
Why did so many walk by?
Were they ashamed?
Were they fearful?
Were they simply in a hurry?
Excuses, excuses, excuses
Stop and help when I ask you
Do what you are able
Open your eyes and see the pain
Open your ears and listen to the silent
cries
Open your heart and let Me enter

Care for Me in the man by the wayside.

~*Luke 6:17-49*~

You are My disciple
I have called you
You are Mine
Do as I did-love
Act as I did-with mercy and
compassion
Heal as I did-with prayer and
sacrifice
Treat all as you would treat Me
Love all with My passion
Be available to those you meet
Be gracious and kind
Be merciful and just
Prepare others to hear My Word
Help them to fathom It
Show them the way to eternity
Let them see Me, not you

~Luke 21:1-4~

Give of yourself
Give time, energy, money
Give of your gifts
Help others see and use their gifts
Give it all back to Me
The glory is Mine alone

~1 John2:12-17~

Be balanced
Be in the world not of it
Be salt and light and savor
Show others My Way
Show others My Love
Help them onto the path
Be filled with joy and peace
Let them know you have the Truth
Be Me to others
Put yourself aside
Accept honor or dishonor in My name
Don't let it get you down
Give all to Me
It is Mine
You are My servant and My slave
Do My work and my will in your
world

~1 John 1:5-10~

You are a sinner
You have repented
You are forgiven
Continue to repent and
Continue to seek reconciliation
I will give you the grace
I am with you on your walk
Slow down and appreciate the view
The scenery is beautiful
Nature can show Me to you
Take it all in

~Psalm 32~

Slow down
Don't allow temptation to become sin
Ask for My help
Trust in Me
I have and will continue to set you free
There is no need to be heavy hearted
Come to Me
I listen, I respond, I forgive and
forget

~Mark 7:1-23~

No one can make you sin
It is an act of your will
Follow My Will
Obey My Commandments
You will be on the correct path

~1 Peter 5:6-11~

The devil is real
He comes in many disguises
Be on guard
Be vigilant
Don't be worried
Follow Me
My Way leads to eternal life
Follow him
You will receive eternal damnation
Which will it be?
Choose with care

~Ephesians 6:10-20~

Hate the sin
Love the sinner
The sinner is under attack
You might be his target
Be firm in your love of Me
Point out the Truth
Show that I Am The Way
I am the light at the end of the tunnel
Bring others to the tunnel
I will draw them in like suction
There is no need to push
Get out of My way.

~Psalm 51~

Keep your heart pure
Don't allow it to harden
Let it beat for Me
Let others see this beating
Let them see your joy
Show them My Mercy
Show them My Way
Your heart is fragile
Put it away from danger
I can reach it
Be open-be vulnerable-be safe

~Psalm 23~

Even when you feel alone or isolated
I am there
I offer you nourishment in the
Eucharist
I offer you forgiveness in Penance
I offer you healing in the Sacrament
of the Sick
You received My Spirit in
Confirmation
At Baptism you were born into Eternal
Life
In Matrimony I gave you a new
family
Use, not abuse all these gift
Share them with others
Be perfect as I am perfect
You have all the graces you need
Use them wisely

~Luke 5:1-11~

Be open to My call
Go where I lead you
Expect the unexpected
You are not responsible for the
outcome
I call many
Lots will not follow
This is their loss
Let them be

~Philippians 3:7-16~

Knowing Me means loving Me
Loving Me means serving Me
Serving Me means following Me
Following Me leads to the cross
After the cross comes the Resurrection
Stay the course

~Philippians 2:1-18~

I didn't say it would be easy
With My help it won't be hard
Salvation is a process
Hold tight to My Truth
Hold tight to My Word
Hold on to Me
Rest in Me
I will rest in you

~2 Corinthians 1:19-20~

Worship Me
I am God
I fulfill all promises
I guide you home
Follow My lead

~John 13:1-15~

I washed feet
Do likewise
Care for all
Don't ask why
Just do it
The reason is not your business if I
have called you
When you become more open to Me
I will show you when and where
Just do it!

~Luke 22:33-46~

Because of My crucifixion and death
You now have a way to Eternal Life
Recall My passion and death
When you are tempted to sin
I will give you peace
Offer yourself with Me
Offer your joys and your sorrows
Lift them up to Me
Pray for others
I have already done the saving work
Share Me with others, gently

~Luke 6:40~

Be My student
Follow Me
Allow Me to instruct you
Persevere and
You will be with Me in Eternity

~1 Corinthians 4:9-13~

I call you to be an apostle
This is no easy task
You will be ridiculed
You will be judged
You will be laughed at
Thank Me
You will be on the right path
Rejoice!

~2 Corinthians 6:1-10~

Tone it down
Your message is too high pitched
Your message is full of static
Put yourself aside
Don't be concerned about yourself
Preach My message
Preach it fully with love
Preach it gently
You will be hurt anyway
Allow Me to absorb most of the pain
It is My message
Don't take the insults personally
Check yourself frequently
If all is in order
Move forward zealously and bravely
Persevere for Me not for you
You will ultimately have inner peace
You will have joy in doing My will
Nothing will bother you
Start anew
Try it-you'll like it
Change for Me
Thank you

~Mark 10:29,30~

Give yourself to Me
Receive all I offer you
You are Mine
You are on the road of Eternal Life
You will be blessed
You will be cursed
Stay the course
I am with you all the way
I care for and about you
I love you
Sometimes loving hurts
Be at peace
Persevere

~Mark 6:1-8~

There is a time for silence
There is a time to proclaim My Word
Listen-I will let you know
I ask to be known everywhere
This is a missionary activity
Be a missionary
You know your territory
I may extend it
Listen-follow My lead
Show your love for Me and others
Your reward will be great in heaven
Don't be concerned about the now
Be concerned, not worried, about
forever
Go in peace

~Romans 6:8~

**Die to sin
Die to self
Live in Grace
Live in Me**

~Revelation 22:1-25~

I see your desire for the Tree of Life
I am aware of your search
The Garden of Eden was closed
It would not be good for sinful man to
live forever
I Am the Tree of Life
I await you
I await you in the Garden of Paradise
Be reformed
Be conformed to My Will
The Garden will be yours
Simply persevere one step at a time

~Acts 1:6-12~

My Holy Spirit entered you at
Baptism
At Confirmation you recognized that
you were My soldier
You have a mission
Do it
Do it with love
Do it with forgetfulness of self
Do it for the greater good
Look at My Love for you
Hold on to it
Do not depart from My Truth
You are My disciple
You are an intricate part of My plan
Keep in touch with Me for instruction
Be obedient
Be calm
Relax, let go, I Am the Savior
You are My Ginny
Be as a tool in My Hand
As you hold My Hand, I guide you
You need not look ahead
I do this

Don't attempt to remove the fog ahead
I keep you from unnecessary knowing
Mind your own business
Do only your part
Relax-relax-relax
I Am God....There is no other
Come, Follow Me
Peace is yours-accept it-relish it
You can never be too joy filled

This ends the retreat portion of the book. I will continue with more inspired poetry which has the title words found in the text.

Part Two

Trust is love
Do you love Me?
Do you want to be with Me?
Can you follow in My footsteps?
Can you feel and carry My pain?
Are you willing to suffer?
Are you willing to praise?
Do you love your enemies?
Can you pray for all?
Become little
Put your feet in My steps
Put your hands in My side
Praise, don't curse
See all as coming from Me
I allow all to come to you
You will not need to understand
You only need to follow and obey
Look for My peace in the midst of
pain
Allow Me to comfort you
Don't stray from the path
I am Love. I love all. Believe

I follow in Your footsteps
They are large and easy to see
You stop and turn and greet me
You offer me Your hand
You invite me to walk beside You
You want me to be Your friend
You guide me through the brambles
You walk with me in the fog
You never let go of my hand
I let go of Yours
You allow me to stumble and fall
You wait patiently for me to call to
You
You never leave me nor forsake me
I leave You, forsake You and sin
You wait patiently for me to call to
You
I am covered with mud and water
You continue inviting me
I am tired-worn out-in pain
I call out and repent
You forgive Me and I see Your
extended hand

Come, listen to Me
Unblock the ears of your heart
Hear Me in the depths of your soul
Allow Me permanent residence there
Speak often to others of Me
Tell them of My love and mercy
Fill yourself with Me
Be at peace

Peace is yours
It is inside
It is in your heart
Listen to Me
Follow My lead
Stay the path
I will clear it for you
Proceed slowly
There is no need to hurry
I will wait for you

Is it signs you want?
I have shown you many
Have you shown any gratitude?
Why would you desire more?
You haven't even looked
At the gifts I have already bestowed
on you
They are left unopened and unused
The ones you have used have been
taken for granted
Open your eyes
See what I have bestowed on you
Be thankful
I will shower you with more
Close your eyes
I will withdraw what I have already
sent
What do you want?
Follow Me and keep all your senses
Open and aware and thankful

Feel My pain
Come and talk with Me about it
Is your pain similar?
Do you hurt everywhere?
Can you identify the cause?
I will listen to your cry
I will show you how to identify with
Me
I will tell you more of Mine
I carried all your sin and your pain
I suffered and died for you
Are you willing to share yours with
Me?
Are you willing to help others by
offering your pain?
Do you think you can identify?
I love you
Some pain can be alleviated
Some pain must be carried
Carry your pain with the grace I offer
to you.
Don't waste it and time complaining
Ask Me for help
Seek the proper counsel
Take the necessary medication and
precautions

Do what you can on a natural level
Then, leave it to Me
I will help you carry it
I will offer you solace in the pain
I am here for you
In your pain you may think of Me
more often
Lift up your heart to Me
I will take your burdens
But
You may still need to carry your pain

COME HOME!!!!

I speak to you in silence
I speak loud and clear
I invite you to be My bride
I call you to purity and holiness
Follow Me
I will lead you home
I will lead you to the right path
I will show you My way
You must be little to follow Me
You must rid yourself of all baggage
You are not aware of your fear
I will reveal it to you
I will show you how to discard it
I will make you whole
You must cooperate

Come hither
I will speak to you
I will speak to you of My love
My love is endless
It spirals out to encompass all

All are not interested
Accept My love and pass it on
One by one all might see Me
Come closer
Listen to Me
I call day and night
I show you My way
I deliver you from all evil
Follow closely
Attach yourself to Me
Do not let Me go
Find more time to speak of Me
Show others Me by your love
Soften your words
Limit your words
Say what I ask of you
And
I will give you rest

I have risen from the dead
I come to you in Holy Communion
You are a part of My Body
Love as I do
Share as I do
Transform the world
Bring your friends to Me
Follow My lead
Don't fall asleep
If you do-wake up
There are many ways to love
Love in deed and in truth
Don't be startled
Show My wounds and My crown
Today it is a crown of glory
Share, share, and then share more
Pray, pray, then pray more
I show you My way
Stay on the path
Others will join you
When
They know where you are going
Strike up the band
Pick up the baton
The parade is about to begin

I am at the head of the Parade, not
you
Use your megaphone
Point Me out to others
I will be transfigured in their eyes
I do all the work
All you need do is praise Me
Come, let us begin

Keep an open mind
Keep an open heart
Fill them with My love
Search and you will find Me
Follow and I will lead
Enjoy My rest and My peace
Smell My flowers
Relax in My tender arms

If you follow Me , I will lead
I you obey Me, I will refresh
I you sing, I will accompany
If you sin, I will hurt
I you love, I did and will die
If you cherish, I will enfold
If you hurt, I will cry
I am here for you
And
So are the members of My body

Come to Me all you who labor
I will give you rest
I comfort and console you
I love and enfold you
I seek your peace
I offer My pain
I died for you
Will you suffer with Me?
Will you care for others?
Will you show them My Love?
Will you stop straying?
Honor and adore Me
Live your life for Me
Pray for those I send to you
Live a life of grace
Look into My face
Share your burdens and your cares
Listen to the pain of others
Help them with its release
Share Me with them
Both of you will find My peace
It is available for the asking
It is free - a gift
Enjoy It – Go forth in My Love

Hearken to My call
Listen to My voice
Obey My orders
Hell is real
Only the damned go there
Share your faith
Keep My commands
Follow My lead
My way leads to Heaven
Heaven should be home
I call everyone
Everyone does not listen
Everyone does not obey
Everyone does not follow
Wake up
Time is of the essence
Desire to seek My glory
Desire to do My will
Desire heaven
Love Me – Love your neighbor
Stay away from sin
Repent and you will live

~Ephesians 6:11~

Be a warrior for Christ
Take Him as your Savior
Read His Word
Follow His teachings
Be prepared always for battle
When it arrives – Call on Him
He will be there for you
Believe

~Romans 8:5-10, 15-17

My Spirit will testify to you
Live in My love
Live in My peace
Live without fear
Come into My arms
I will give you rest

~John 15:9-14~

Be My friend
Keep My commandments
Follow My lead and live

All things are new
The old is gone
I have buried it
Come, see the beauty
Look closely at Me
I am all you need
Find Me in others
Let go of all else
Renew – Re-vigor - Resuscitate

I help you because you ask
I help you even when you forget to ask
I am always with you
I care about you
My concern goes very deep
Do not fear
I am in control — You are not
Be prepared to offer thanks
Come, follow Me
Relax into My love
Fear not
Let go of anger and resentment
Leave them with Me
Be cleansed of all concerns of the mind
and body
Go forth in My peace
Love - Love - Love

My heart is open
Fill it with Your Love
Lead me to Your side
Protect me from all sin
Let me set aside illusion
Show me reality
Call Me and I will follow
Allow me to rest in Your heart
Forever

I see you
Look at Me
Praise Me
Adore Me
Worship Me
I see your heart
See Mine
It beats for you
I am alive
I live
I come to you
Visit Me
I long for you
Come closer
I see your eyes
Be a reflection of Mine
Be at peace
I bring peace
I am peace
Follow Me
I will lead you home
I will show you My way
Live and love in Me

Seek My face
Adore Me
Memorize My Love
I treasure you
Follow My lead
I show you My Way
Don't get lost
Stay on the path
If you should stray
Call on Me
I will once again show you My Way
You are special
I offer you light and love and peace
Accept My gifts
Offer them to others

You are a living stone
You are a part of My temple
You live in Me
I alone can move you
Don't attempt to move on your own
You will be seriously injured
Follow Me
Stay close to Me
Bear the weight I place on you
I carry the entire load
You have a share in the burden
No one can jar you out of place
If you rest firmly on Me
Trust Me – I love you dearly

You are in exile
Earth is temporary for you
You were created for Eternity
Follow Me
I continue to show you My Way
Hunger for Heaven
Do not attempt to be satisfied in the
now

Eternal Life is forever
Accept My challenge
Love for and in Me
Put on the armor of God
Be ready for battle
You have chosen My side
Listen to Me for direction
Follow My lead
Do not look around
The others may not be on My side

There is a hell
It is everlasting
You, alone, make your own decision
Follow Me
Keep on the straight path
When you go off – Repent
Get up and begin again
I love you
I desire Heaven for you
Follow Me
I will give you peace
Do not worry

~2 Corinthians 6:2~

Now is the time
Tomorrow may be too late
Join with Me
Follow My lead
Salvation is at hand
It is My gift to you
And to all who desire
And
Follow Me

~1 Thessalonians 5:8-9~

Salvation is yours
Simply ask
I want all to know Me
All will not follow
Some will lag behind
There is time to catch up
Come - Follow Me
I am the Word of God
I am the Alpha and Omega
Read Me - Digest Me - Listen to Me
Come, Follow Me
My Word is Love and Truth
My Word is for all time
My Word shows the Way
I Am the Way
Come, Follow Me

Trust in Me
I will never disappoint
Believe in Me
I Am the All in All
Have faith in Me
I am a strong tower
Love Me
I will love others through you
Pray to Me
I hear and always answer
Obey Me
I never ask more than you can give
Follow Me
I will lead you home

Anticipate Me
I wait for you
I hold your hand
I enfold you in My embrace
I dry your tears
I know your needs
Tell Me all
I already know all
I will fill all your needs
It may not be the way you expected
Expect the unexpected
I am always with you
You are My child
All My children are held closely
Wait for Me
Do not rush forward
Move slowly and gracefully
Rome wasn't built in a day
I still have much work to do in you
You must be still and stop struggling
Relax – I am in control
Leave all to Me
And
You will be surprised at the results

Continue to be child-like
Be open to others
Expect nothing
Give everything
Never shun any one
Only I know their hearts
Continue to be open and receptive
Allow Me to hold any rejection
Never intentionally offend
Follow My lead
Back off if you are not greeted
Let others have the freedom to leave
Follow My lead
Don't push - or pull
Be open, receptive, and pure
Don't allow yourself to spiral down
Love all with My love
This will make every encounter easy
Be a free spirit
Bring joy with the truth
Allow the truth to settle
Don't settle yourself with less
Come, Follow Me
I appreciate your childlikeness

Ask anything of Me
I will answer
I hear your call
I know your voice
Do you know Mine?
I call in the desert
Does anyone hear Me?
I call from the mountain top
Does anyone listen?
Keep your ears open
Keep your heart open
Tell your friends
Invite them to listen
Come, I will speak

On April 29, 1949, I wrote the following poem inspired by _The Selfish Giant_ by Oscar Wilde. My untitled poem has remained in my memory all these years. Recently I found the original.

I seem to see the sun go down
Beneath that shady tree
That once upon a time to me
It was so light and bright
In summer sun and winter snow
That tree to me was still as light as was before
Because that tree, the tree that I loved,
Was the tree where Our Lord sat in the Garden of Paradise

Biography

I'm Virginia (for the Virgin Mary), Carol (for Christmas carol), Justine (after my father and brother and the martyr), Kearney (my maiden name), Allen (my married name), an extrovert on natural or spiritual steroids. Just call me Ginny. Presently I live near the beach in Kennebunk, Maine.

I was a desired child by both of my parents and was born by Caesarian section on December 23, 1939, after a difficult labor which caused me to have stitches on my side. I had to fight to stay alive and thus have always been a fighter or a feisty person. I choose to believe that I was conceived on the feast of the Annunciation.

On January 14, 1940 I was baptized and became a child of God. Seven years later, I made my First

Confession and on May 10, 1947, my First Communion. My confession was heard by all the other kids. Even then, I spoke loudly. I was now on my way. These sacraments were serious business!

In my Baltimore Catechism I was asked "Why was I born?" "I was born to know, love and serve God in this world and be happy with Him forever in heaven." This has always been my operating mission statement. I never wanted to commit a mortal sin because I never wanted to miss my goal or go to hell.

The time of childhood through college graduation was rather smooth. My passion and zeal were sometimes stifled but I always managed to pop up again. I had fun! I enjoyed life! My father was my hero and my spiritual role model and the one who admonished me. He was the spiritual head of our home. In 1950 I was confirmed. I became a soldier of Christ. This was really heady!

I attended Mass every Sunday, went to confession regularly, sat through an annual mission, was considered a prude but did nothing extra in the church. For ten years I attended Catholic school and really loved my Catholic faith and its rules which I saw as black and white. Things were not and are not gray, to me at all. I was not invisible! A few years ago, in a conversation with my high school friend Ted, I was reminded that I was always religious.

After Daddy died, shortly following college graduation, I spent a year as a dietetic intern in the Big Apple. If it hadn't been for my Daddy's daily prayer, "Jesus, Mary and Joseph, guide and guard and love and protect Ginny. Mary, Queen of Purity, watch over her", I might have allowed my sin nature to have full reign. He was gone. I, however, recognized my adult responsibility to God. My Daddy's prayer got me through that year unscathed. My Daddy's prayer still gets me through each day. His prayer has now been passed on to my children and grandchildren.

Upon returning home, I spent a year as a fun loving, vivacious, risk-taking single. I went on a couple of terrific vacations, all the while in search of the perfect husband. As far back as I can remember I wanted to be a wife and mother. I hadn't yet found the man God had chosen for me.

On December 28, 1963 I received the sacrament of Matrimony. In addition to the usual vows, Jim and I had a special goal. We would procreate and educate, through college, whatever number of children God sent. The fun loving girl sort of began hibernating. I was no longer a free agent. I had responsibilities! These were awesome!

I was a part of God's plan! This sacrament was serious business!

I put the fun aside! Skiing was one of the really freeing experiences I had enjoyed. I was afraid of breaking an arm or a leg and not being able to care for my family. I gave skiing and other risky adventures up willingly. I believed we needed to save money for whatever number of college educations were in the future. We were very thrift conscious. My degree was being put to good use. Most of our social life revolved around the church. We also attended many dances. Dancing and singing are two of my favorite pastimes. The rhythm is in me!

Jim and I believed in our long range goal. I was happy! My friends from that period of my life would attest that I was a very submissive wife. During this time I did some CCD teaching and was a lector. My passion showed itself in my caring about my children and those of others. I was passionate for the courses they took and I looked deeply into the curriculum especially in areas of sex and drug education. With five children and a husband to care for, I had little time for much else. I was the "Country Bunny and the Little Gold Shoes" as depicted by Du Bose Heyward, except that there were tears at times in our, "little country cottage", family. My voice was not always calm and gentle and quiet. My love was tough when it needed to be as I was raising children for God. I believe in the biblical admonition to instruct and admonish.

My next phase began when my youngest was four years old. I was invited to a non-denominational Bible study. I came to know Jesus in a deep, personal way! I went from not doing something because it might cause me to land in hell (attrition) to not doing it because it hurt God (contrition). Prior to this I never could understand how I could offend God who is all good and deserving of all my love. WOW!!! I was on fire! I began attending daily Mass as often as I could. I became very involved in Bible study which has continued until this day. Because I was studying with mostly non-Catholics I asked God to define my ministry He let me know it is to former Catholics. He uses me to invite them to return to the faith of their childhood. I have taken this very seriously. In the past few years I have been evangelizing at the beach and wherever my watercolors with Bible verses on them take me. These are business card sized and easily put on a refrigerator or in a wallet.

I have kept up to date on the teachings of the Roman Catholic Church and have been very passionate about this. I now have much free time. God graces me with poetry on a regular basis and I share this with others. I have previously printed one book,

<u>Broken and Bruised, Holy and Sanctified</u>, and distributed over 500 copies.

A few years ago, when visiting Shirley, I received the Sacrament of the Sick a day before I was hospitalized in an emergency. God knew what I did not. This accounts for all the six sacraments which I am allowed to receive. I have never been a feminist and never wanted to receive the seventh sacrament of Holy Orders. I am blessed!

Recently, I went on my first silent retreat. It was hard work. The work continues. Another phase of my life has begun. God has given me direction. I have written this book. He has freed me from regular responsibility and is asking me to once again have fun. I don't really know what this is for me. Wait and see what unfolds!

Books I have enjoyed and reread over the years… no particular order

The Bible

Man's Search for Meaning~Viktor Frankl

The Country Bunny and the Little Gold Shoes~Dubose Heyward

Imitation of Christ~Thomas a Kempis

The Art of Living~Dietrich and Alice von Hildebrand

The Little House~Virginia Lee Burton

A Child's Garden of Verses~Robert Louis Stevenson

The Race~Dee Groberg

AA-1025~Marie Carre

Preparation For Death~St. Alphonsus
De Liguroi

Hind's Feet on High Places~Hannah
Hurnard

Abandonment to Divine
Providence~Jean-Pierre de Caussade

Will Many Be Saved~Ralph Martin

Introduction to the Devout
Life~Francis de Sales

The Secret Garden~Frances Hodgson
Burnett

Heidi Johanna Spyri

Consoling the Heart of Jesus~Michael
E. Gaitley, MIC

Seeking Spiritual Direction~Thomas
Dubay, S.M.

Fire Within~Thomas Dubay, S.M.

The Discernment of Spirits~Timothy
M. Gallagher, OMV

Spiritual Consolation~Timothy M.
Gallagher, OMV

The Fulfillment of all Desire~Ralph
Martin

The Cloud of Unknowing~Anonymous

Abandonment to Divine
Providence~J.P. de Caussade, S.J.

Made in the USA
San Bernardino, CA
28 September 2013